DRUGS EXPLAINED

the real deal on alcohol, pot, ecstasy, and more

DRUGS EXPLAINED

the real deal on alcohol, pot, ecstasy, and more

Pierre Mezinski
with Melissa Daly and Françoise Jaud
illustrated by Redge

Library of Congress Cataloging-in-Publication data:
Mezinski, Pierre.
Drugs explained : the real deal on alcohol, pot, ecstasy, and more /
Pierre Mezinski, with Melissa Daly and Françoise Jaud ; illustrated by
Redge; Sunscreen.
p. cm.
Includes bibliographical references and index.
ISBN 0-8109-4931-8
1. Substance abuse. 2. Drug abuse. I. Daly, Melissa. II. Jaud,
Françoise. III. Title.
HV4998.M49 2004
362.29—dc22
2004012563

Text copyright © 2004 Pierre Mezinski with Melissa Daly
and Françoise Taud
Illustrations © 1999, 2004 Redge
Book series design by Higashi Glaser Design
Translated by Paul Hurwit

Published in 2004 by Amulet Books
an imprint of Harry N. Abrams, Incorporated
100 Fifth Avenue
New York, NY 10011
www.abramsbooks.com

Abrams is a subsidiary of

LA MARTINIÈRE
GROUPE

contents

phase 2:

THE BIG QUESTIONS

phase 3:

THE DRUG DEBATE

WHAT'S THE
BIG DEAL?
WHAT DO DRUGS
DO, EXACTLY?
WHAT IF A
FRIEND HANDS
ME A CIGARETTE?
HOW DO I
SAY NO WITH-
OUT SEEMING
LIKE A LOSER?

The use of drugs probably dates back to prehistoric times. Archaeologists believe that primitive peoples used plants to heal the body and also to alter the mind. On Timor, an island in southeastern Asia, a narcotic called the betel nut has been chewed for its relaxing effects for thousands of years. Marijuana use appears in two-thousand-year-old Chinese records. But it wasn't until the second half of the twentieth century that the terms "habit" and "addiction" sprang up to refer to the habitual use or abuse of these and other drugs. Now abuse has become so widespread that drugs have emerged as a real plague on young people in industrialized countries—a plague that threatens teenagers who feel out of place or on the fringe, as well as those who just like to try new things, or to whom anything that's against the rules automatically seems more attractive.

So how about you? The day someone—with either good or bad intentions—offers you something meant to help you have more fun, or to relax you, or to put you at ease, or to make you feel like one of the crowd, what will you answer? To make the best decision, you'll need to be knowledgeable. As you read Emily's journal on the following pages, you'll watch her experience situations that you may have already encountered, or might soon in the future. You'll see how she handles all the questions that come up, and you can compare that with the way you might do things.

In the sections that follow Emily's journal, you will find information on various types of drugs, how they work, and the potential risks involved with each.

november

EMILY'S

still
in
april

MAY

june

DECEMBER

march

january

april

february

JOURNAL

JULY

november

It's raining, it's cold, it's disgusting. And I'm bored to death. Although, it's not like it'd be any different if the sun were blazing away. I'm bored in any kind of weather. Mom always says I've got everything I need to be happy. That's probably why I'm so bored.

I'm thirteen and a half years old, which gives me about another seventy years of this... But maybe I won't have to worry about filling up all that time—at this rate, I'll probably die really young... OF BOREDOM.

Dad's always saying, "With all the money we spend on your activi-ties! You should take advantage of them, or maybe we won't keep paying for it all!" Then Mom joins the fun: "I wish I'd been as lucky as you! When I was younger I would have killed to take piano lessons!"

It's no use pointing out to her that that's the whole problem right there: I am ab-so-lute-ly fed up with doing scales day in and day out because SHE used to dream about being a musician. And the result of all this is that after four years, I know how to butcher three classical pieces.

"If you worked a little harder, you'd be able to learn something new." She won't quit! "But you never open the piano. It's such a beautiful instrument!"

Then she's off again for another round: when *she* was my age ... blah, blah, blah, blah, blah.

I'm sick of karate, too, which is where they send me only because they can take tai-chi down the hall at the same time. Karate was supposed to give me strength and self-confidence. So why am I still not allowed to go out at night without a chaperone? Hello?! Anyway, I really have no desire to learn how to beat people up. I'm a girl, not the next Karate Kid.

Then there's the outfit. Seriously, I look like a big, fat, barefoot chef in it. Not flattering.

OK, OK, I admit it: I was the one who asked to take karate in the first place. But that was a million years ago, back when I was all tomboyish. Don't I have the right to change my mind?

Today, though, I've come to terms with myself. I'm not into all that kid stuff anymore. But no one here cares. Dad's always stressed about work, since people are getting laid off left and right at his company and Mom's got a really hard class of kids this year (she's an English teacher). That's all she thinks and talks about, and she has these really bad nightmares about it. When she manages to forget her class for five minutes, she just worries about Jeremy (my eight-year-old brother). Since the time in the middle of the night when they carted him off to the hospital because of his burst appendix, he's become like the family superhero, the little darling, the one everyone loves. It's too bad the doctors didn't surgically remove his tongue instead of his appendix. "Mom, Em took your perfume . . . Mom, Em didn't make her bed . . . Em didn't walk Ulysses!"

Our dog, Ulysses, has to have a long walk around the lake every morning and every night, so he can stretch his legs. And who's the one who has the honor of doing this chore? OK, I'm exaggerating. I love my puppy! He's the only one who thinks I'm his entire world. We got him a million years ago; he was just a big bunch of black curly hair with paws too big for his body. We've grown up together, and I've walked him thousands of times. But that's just it, the walk around the lake, that freakin' walk around the lake! It's so boring and annoying, it's turning my brain to mush.

I don't know why, but everything is just bugging me so much lately. Even Stephanie, my best friend since forever. Sometimes I can't stand her anymore. She never has any problems, everything always works out perfectly for her. She actually *likes* piano lessons. She wants to be a lawyer like her dad—that is, if that's what her mom and dad want her to do. If not, she'll just do whatever they say! She's got about as much imagination as my left shoe. OK, I guess I'm being too mean. Right now she's all shaken up because her parents are getting a divorce. But then she claims that it's better this way—at least they'll stop their arguing. That's just like her, always so sugary sweet. It could rain crap, and she'd go around saying it was good for the farmers.

It's not any better at school. In my class, all the boys are babies. As for the girls, let's see . . . you've got the Stephanie type—the nice, pleasant, twin-set-wearing Goody Two-shoes who's been raised very properly. Then there are the others, dressed all in black, or really tight clothes, or oversized clothes, with tall, clunky boots or three-inch heels.

Well, I'm in the mix somewhere, too, but I just want to be myself— not a type. Who that is exactly . . . sometimes I'm not sure.

december

I AM FURIOUS. I have the worst parents in the world! Stephanie's brother invited me to a party that a bunch of eighth-graders are throwing at the end of the quarter. Seventh-graders aren't supposed to go, but of course we're all dying to. So, shockingly, I actually get asked—but I still can't go! They never budge: "No, sweetie, you're too young." Instead, on the day of the party, I'll be busy sitting on my butt in the ski lodge, while Mom and Dad hit the slopes.

According to Stephanie—who, by the way, is secretly hurt that she wasn't invited—it's better this way. Because it's the kind of party where boys try to pick up girls, everybody drinks, and some people even smoke

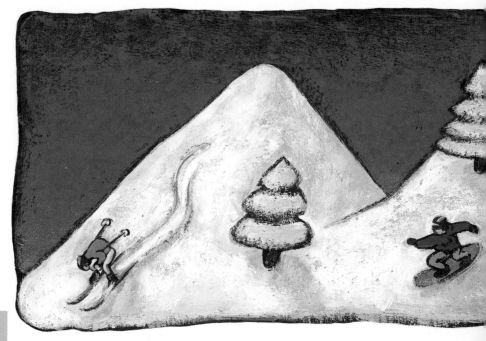

pot. But I said, "So what? Are you scared I'll try it?" Like the sheep she is, she started bleating with righteous indignation. It's not like I'm going to be sucked in by some evil druggy, like my parents seem to think. It's always the same: Maybe when I'm fourteen, but right now I'm too young to go to a party with a guy. What are the odds that I'll be allowed to stay home alone or even at a friend's house while the family goes skiing? None, zero, zip.

It's ridiculous. They can't even see that it would be convenient for them. They're the ones who love these ski weekends; I hate being away from my friends for two days. I hate the cold, the snow, the mountains, the lodges, the skiers, even the pine trees. It really doesn't matter that a lot of people would love to take my place—please do, be my guest! I have no desire to go.

january

the weirdest thing happened: There were *two* new kids in school, both on the same day—a guy and a girl. It's really odd that they came at the same time, since they're not brother and sister or anything like that. In fact, no one really knows anything about them, where they come from or why they just came out of nowhere to a new school in the middle of the year, or even why they're in seventh grade when they look like they're old enough to be in eighth or ninth.

Eleanor, the girl, is pretty annoying so far. She looks down at us like she's wondering what rat hole she's fallen into. She doesn't talk to anyone, and she copies everything the teachers say like some neurotic suck-up. I'd say she's at least fifteen. We haven't spoken yet. It bugs me that she probably thinks of me as just one of the little brats like everyone else.

The guy's name is David, and he's gorgeous! SO cute. Cuter than any of the other guys here, at least. He's tall, strong, has beautiful eyes and this sort of aloof attitude that actually makes him even more adorable.

Stephanie, who knows everyone, went to investigate. From the daughter of one of our teachers, she learned that David is from New York City and that he just moved in with his grandparents here. The teachers talked about some "problems" that he supposedly had at his last school. Whatever happened, it's obviously the reason he had to leave right in the middle of the year. "Problems" could mean anything, though. But it probably doesn't matter, anyway. There's no chance he'll notice me amid the growing flock of girls already throwing themselves at his feet.

february

Today we had a big assembly in the auditorium about drugs. It was two hours long and I got to sit next to David the whole time! He even talked to me! Actually, he never *stopped* talking. I still haven't recovered from the shock. The program began with the introduction of the speakers—the nurse who leads the Health Club, the guidance counselor, a psychologist who works for a drug addiction prevention network, and two youth workers who lead a school group that helps kids with those kinds of problems.

The nurse began by talking about substances that are classified as drugs. She said that the most widely used drug at our age is tobacco. A few people smirked when she said it, I guess because they knew what she was talking about, or because they don't really think of tobacco as a drug. She was right, though—there's a group you always see smoking on the other side of the parking lot after school, like they can barely wait for class to end to get off school grounds and light up.

Anyway, then the nurse started talking about alcohol and marijuana. David suddenly began to squirm in his chair, sneer a little nervously, and say things through clenched teeth. So I asked him what was up, and he launched into his whole life story.

Before he ended up here, David was living in Manhattan with his mother and stepfather. It wasn't going well. He didn't say much about

it, but I got the feeling he just couldn't stand to be with his family, or at school, anymore. The school sounded pretty bad. Apparently the teachers just couldn't control the kids, so they pretty much had free rein to do whatever they wanted. He started to cut classes, and when he did show up, a lot of times it was in what they called a "strange condition." One day he couldn't sit still and the next he'd be practically falling asleep. They even had to take him to the infirmary a few times. So eventually they called his mom, and finally they discovered that he'd been smoking pot before school with his older buddies. He was like: "Talk about making a huge production over a few joints! My mom, I could easily have calmed down; but my stepfather, he was just waiting for a reason to throw me out. All he cared about was that I was setting a bad example for the kids—my stepbrothers. He said the only way to get me to stop hanging out with my 'delinquent' friends was to send me away. So my grandparents took me in. They looked around to find the best school for me and found out that this place has a club that's supposed to help kids with drug problems. So here I am. But what did they think was going to happen, I'd just become a

different person overnight? I hadn't been here even two days and I already knew who was selling what. It's really not hard to find. Old people always think they understand everything better than everyone else, but they can't even see what's right there under their noses. Look at that old bag over there—she doesn't have a clue what she's talking about! She's probably never even tried it!"

He was pointing at the nurse, who was in the middle of an explanation about inhalants. Apparently, you can get high just by breathing certain substances used in cleaning products and stuff. She was saying it's one of the most dangerous things you can do, because the solvents cause major damage to the brain and can put you into a coma the first time you do it.

When the assembly was almost over, the youth workers, Karim and Sophie, started talking. They were plugging the school support group, called The Right Path. They have a room in the guidance office where they help kids do their homework after school. Sophie's a sophomore in college and training to become a teacher. Karim is getting his associate's degree in math. "In principle," Sophie said, laughing, "signing up for The Right Path is completely voluntary. In reality, we end up seeing mainly kids who are dragged in by their parents or teachers. But if anyone's interested, don't hesitate to stop by."

As it turns out, David is one of the kids being dragged in. So I think I'll sign up, too! Karim and Sophie seem pretty cool; they're not like teachers who you dread asking for help. And it's better than doing homework at home. And, of course, the best part: I'll have the chance to talk to David more!

march

Things are finally starting to get good around here. Since I've been going to The Right Path, lots of things have changed. Even Mom and Dad are amazed, and they're treating me a little less like a baby. It's actually the first time I've had the chance to really talk about certain things with people, stuff Stephanie wouldn't understand.

She thinks she's too good and pure to need The Right Path.

Karim is really a good guy. He's the one I talk with, mostly. He's told me where he's from and how he got here. He was born in a pretty bad part of the city. When he was a teenager, he went through a rough period when he was always getting into fights. They had to practically bullwhip him to get him to class. All he wanted was to just tag along behind his "big brothers," the guys who were "real" and tough, the ones who always seemed to have something interesting going on. People at school used to tell him all the time that he was wasting his potential, especially one math teacher who sensed he had talent and hated seeing the direction he was headed in. In the end, though, it was one really dramatic event that turned his life around. Seven years ago, his real big brother, Mustapha, died from a heroin overdose.

His parents didn't know anything about his brother shooting up. Now they're devastated. Karim was thirteen when it happened. He was really depressed for a while and thought he'd never be the same again. But then he started to feel angry about it, and that helped him fight back, first for himself, then for others. He started to hit the books, hard. He got his high school diploma, then went to college so he could get a science scholarship. He wants kids to stop thinking that the older guys who take drugs, go to prison, and end up ruining themselves or other people are heroes. Mustapha had been HIV-positive from using an infected needle, but he died before he got AIDS. Karim has this gnawing suspicion that his overdose may have been some kind of suicide in disguise, so he could end things once and for all before he got really sick. Whatever happened, you can tell Karim has a personal score to settle with drug dealers. He can't stand them.

There's a guy who hangs out around the club room named William. He's seventeen, and the others told me that he's been dealing for years, out in the open—well, sort of. He started by selling sleeping pills and tranquilizers that he lifted straight from his mom's medicine cabinet. He sold them for two dollars a pill and made a fortune. Then he moved on to selling pot. He'll often slide up to the door at The Right Path just to annoy Karim. Karim can't stand him. "Guys like that are garbage," he says. "All they're after is money, any way they can get it. His mom works night and day cleaning houses just to support him. She tries so hard, but what can she do with scum like him?"

Karim's really worried about Alex, a boy who comes to The Right Path because he's in danger of having to repeat seventh grade. He's a strange guy: doesn't say anything, kind of jumps around inside his skin. He wears pants that literally hang off him, and sweatshirts that are three sizes too big. I've heard he locks himself in his room at home, pulls the shades down, and sits in the dark for hours. His mom's worried. She's the one who pushed him into joining the club. But it's not much use. He comes in, sits down in a corner, and watches the clock till it's over. Never says a word to Karim or Sophie. They do what they can to get him to participate. But I think they're just doing it so they can tell themselves they tried, not because they think they'll succeed.

Karim is really ticked off because he saw William talking to Alex a few times in the doorway. William seems to have a way of zeroing in on kids like Alex. He senses they're totally vulnerable, so it'd be pretty easy to turn them into new customers. Karim seems to know everything about everyone here, so he must know that Alex has a lot of money. His mother gives him as much as he wants.

april

David was incredible today! It was because of him that we had a really interesting debate at school.

The Health Club's still waging its war on drugs. This time, they presented a play about it. It was the story of a group of friends who want to start a band. There was a girl on keyboards who really knew how to play.

Anyway, in the scene, everything was going well at first; then Freddy, the guitarist, began playing really badly and acting all strange. His friends were worried: they thought he must be having some problems, but they didn't know what. Once, the keyboardist saw him downing a bottle of whiskey. Another time, she found a syringe.

At that point, the actors stopped acting and asked us to invent the conclusion. Did someone have to talk to Freddy? Who? And what were they supposed to say? How could anybody help him? They asked for someone to go up on stage and play the part of one of his friends. No one moved. But finally, David stepped up. He ran up on stage and delivered a long speech to the guitarist on the theme: "Don't drink, don't stick yourself with needles, you'll ruin your gift, etc., etc." But then, just when they thought he was finished, he blurted out: "Just be happy

smoking a few joints. It won't do you any harm and it'll relax you!"

Everyone burst out laughing, with some yelling, applause, and a few protests. Eleanor (the new girl) stood up and asked David if he bought his marijuana at the corner store. She was yelling: "Pot may not be heroin, but you still have to go to a sketchy dealer who might sell you any junk at all, stuff laced with rat poison or something. You never know what you could end up with."

David immediately shot back that that was exactly the reason that they should legalize marijuana, so you could buy it right at the nice, safe corner store. After all, it's a lot less dangerous than alcohol, which leads to thousands of drunk-driving accidents and can cause alcohol poisoning. "But, of course, alcohol is something adults enjoy, so they'd never prohibit that!"

Eleanor wasn't going to let herself be torn down like that, so she replied: "But it's not the adults you see stumbling home from parties all trashed every Friday night and waking up the next day half-dead!" A wave of laughter broke over the room. Everyone was only too aware of what she was talking about. David's adrenaline must have been going full-blast, because he shot back that if they smoked pot, they wouldn't put themselves in a condition like that. Then the discussion exploded in all directions. So the actor who played Freddy took up his guitar and started playing again. The others, too, grabbed their instruments. Gradually, everyone stopped talking since they couldn't hear themselves over the song. After that, the debate started again, but it was calmer.

When I got home, I opened the piano and tried to figure out the song they played from memory. Mom stuck her head in, pretty surprised and happy to hear me playing. It might sound dumb, especially since my playing really didn't sound good at all, but for some reason it made me happy, too.

still in april

David was acting really weird today. He laughed at everything (whether it was funny or not). His eyes were red and he looked all dazed. He would start talking about something, lose his train of thought, then just break down laughing. I asked him what was going on. He just stuttered out something incoherent.

ph1

When we went into class, I was afraid he'd act like an idiot. He settled in the back of the class and quietly fell asleep. At least he kept himself from snoring. The teacher, who was overjoyed at finally having some calm, didn't notice anything—or at least she pretended not to. By gym class, David had recovered. He was almost normal. We actually walked to The Right Path together. I was delirious about getting to spend time alone with him, but then the moment we arrived, William and Alex showed up and David left me on my own and went off to hang out with them. I wasn't about to join them, because William disgusts me. But at the same time I wanted to follow them to stay with David. I'm not stupid, I knew what they were probably going to do. It felt like David was headed some place and I couldn't follow because I couldn't keep up—or didn't really want to . . . I wasn't sure. But then Karim came out of the

room and called to me. I think he saw David bound away like a cartoon rabbit. He wasn't too pleased. But he didn't say anything. He just asked me if I could help Eleanor, who was having trouble with our French homework. Not that Eleanor seemed too excited about that idea. I don't know why, but that girl can't stand the sight of me. Since I started talking to David, she's been sending lots of nasty looks in my direction. But I know it's not jealousy, because she doesn't like him. She always has something mean to say to him. And to me, too, and it always hits the mark. This time it was: "So you're hanging out with dealers, now? Really bright." Then she lectured me that William was known for being very nice to cute young girls who would pay him back for their drugs—but not with money. I just blew her off. I told her she could do her French on her own. Then to top it all off, I was the one who got in trouble with Karim for it. It's so annoying, but it's always like that. I don't know why he and Sophie have endless amounts of forgiveness for Eleanor. They claim she's had a tough life and she's trying really hard to make up for the time she's lost. But she would have been better off if she'd just worked harder earlier, then she wouldn't still be in seventh grade at her age!

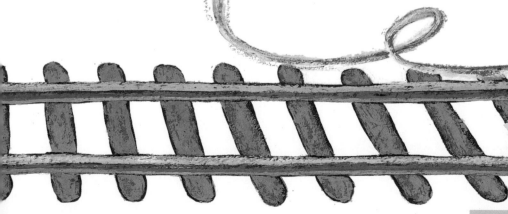

may

I'm sick of The Right Path. David doesn't even go anymore, and I don't think he'll ever come back. It's been awful there ever since Alex's mother came to complain. She came flying through the door one day in a complete meltdown, yelling that her son had become a junior criminal since he started coming for after-school help. Alex was always asking for money. If she said no, he helped himself to her purse anyway. That had never happened before he began hanging around here.

Karim and Sophie knew immediately what was happening. So later, when they heard William's moped backfire outside, they went out to talk to him. They threatened to report him to his social worker, but he just laughed. Since he'd already had run-ins with the law and he was still a minor, he'd been under the supervision of a social worker for years. Result: nada. So Karim and Sophie said they would call the police then— Alex's mother was ready to file a complaint. Alex stayed off to the side this whole time, as though none of it was his concern. David was the one who pounced

on the situation. He was furious. He started insulting Karim and Sophie, calling them narcs, informers. After all that, he left with William, swearing he would never set foot in the place again.

Alex didn't come back again, either. We found out a social worker had met with his parents and had recommended he see a psychologist.

Anyway, the main result for me is that I never get to see David anymore. At school, he comes or he doesn't, whatever he feels like doing. When he's there, he either sleeps or picks fights. The teachers are fed up, I can tell. He's going to end up being kicked out. That's probably what he wants. I wish there was something I could do, but he doesn't even talk to me anymore.

june

At last, good news—extremely good news! The first thing is that the school year is over and I'm officially in eighth grade. "Could have done better" was written all over my report card, but the main thing is, I passed, so Mom and Dad are letting me go to the party the Chamin twins are giving to celebrate the end of the year. (That's the second piece of exciting news.) I can't wait, especially since David is going, too. This may be the last chance I'll have to see him. I have no idea where he'll be over summer vacation. I don't even know if he's coming back to school next year. Because of his grades, all Ds and Fs, they're advising him to undergo some kind of "redirection." He'll probably change schools, and just disappear forever... unless the party gives me the courage to... I don't even know what! I'm sure I'll chicken out and do nothing.

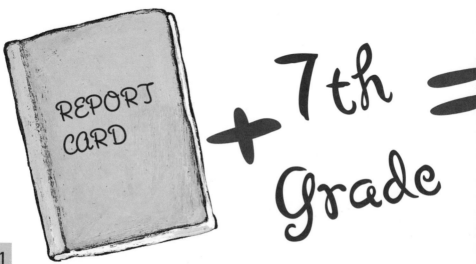

REPORT CARD + 7th Grade =

july

Well, I did much worse than chicken out. I went to the twins' party. But I'd give anything to turn back time and just stay home. I wish I could just erase the whole night.

The twins' parents were away visiting friends, and they'd set up the basement for the party. By the time I got there, everything was ready: the Ping-Pong table had become a buffet table, the lawn chairs were scattered everywhere, the lights were turned down, and the music was playing. Some people had brought drinks.

Everyone was there. I went to say hi to the twins and then started looking for David. He was at the food table with a girl I didn't know. He didn't even say hi. The girl was really pretty and had a lot of makeup on, and her hair was dyed all different colors. I looked like a plain, boring, little girl next to her. Suddenly I just felt so ugly, so nonexistent, that I wanted to go home. If only I'd done that!

To snap out of it, I grabbed a glass off the table. I thought it was orange juice. I drank about half before I realized there was alcohol in it. But, since it wasn't that bad, I finished the whole glass. I wasn't too worried about it. The one time I'd tried alcohol before at a wedding, it tasted terrible. So I was sure there was no chance I'd be able to drink too much. I thought I'd have to force myself to finish another glass. The opposite was true.

"Well, hello there!" said Kevin (one of the twins). "Looks like someone's found a new favorite drink!"

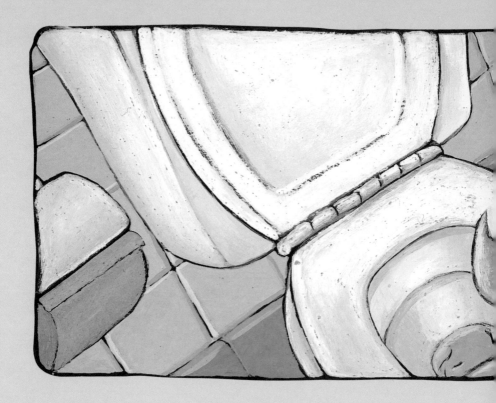

"She's going to be sick for sure. She's not used to it," Eleanor chimed in.

I was so embarrassed and mad at Eleanor I picked up another glass, although the first one was already doing something weird to me. I felt funny, but it wasn't bad-funny. I could feel the liquor radiating heat in my stomach. But at the same time, I didn't feel ugly anymore. I was happy, sure of myself, confident that everything would turn out OK. I laughed really loudly. And I kept drinking.

I'm so ashamed of what happened next. I wish I could just pretend it was all a dream. The worst thing is that I'm not sure I even remember everything right. At some point, I got so drunk that everything got kind of scrambled in my head. All that's left are a few incoherent images. I can

see myself again, dancing all alone like an idiot, then running to the bathroom to throw up, again and again, making disgusting sounds. Melanie (the other twin) came in to see what was going on. She saw me kneeling in front of the bowl, throwing up everything I'd drunk. They took me out, cleaned me up a little, then someone took me into the yard and left me all stretched out there. I must have passed out. The vomiting hadn't sobered me up any; it felt like the opposite. The world was spinning. I couldn't have moved an arm or a leg if my life depended on it.

I don't know how long I lay in the grass. But when I came to, someone was stretched out on top of me. I was so out of it that at first I thought it was David. Only when he started kissing me did I realize who it really was: it was William. He was lying on top of me, feeling me all over with his gross, sticky hands. If the alcohol hadn't turned me so numb, I would have died of horror. But I was so weak, so stunned, that I couldn't even thrash around. I let him do whatever he wanted. I don't know what would have happened if Eleanor hadn't shown up. She grabbed William by the collar and pulled him off me.

"Can't you see she's completely plastered?" she cried. "Leave her alone! You better get back inside—David's going through your bag and he's already swallowed about half of the pills in there."

She left and William ran after her. I got up and straightened myself as well as I could. My head was still spinning. I felt sick and more ashamed than I'd ever been before. I couldn't think straight. I was just thinking that I had to go back to get my jacket and purse before I went home, but couldn't bear to face all those people who had seen me acting so stupid. I saw people coming and going and running everywhere. There was some kind of big commotion going on. I recognized the twins' parents, then I saw an ambulance and men carrying a stretcher. Everything was blurry and fast, making my stomach flip the way it does in a nightmare.

Later I found out what had happened. David had arrived already high. Before the party, he had smoked a lot with William. Then he drank and smoked more once he got to the twins' house. At one point, William had said they should make the party into a real rave. He had some ecstasy that he was selling at a special price for his friends, about half as much as it would normally cost, the highest-quality stuff, just what this party needed. But Eleanor put a stop to that. She totally went off on him, so no one took him up on his offer. Later, when William was outside with me, David took the pills out of his bag and told everyone, "Look, I'll test the stuff for you!"

He swallowed one pill, which didn't seem to have any effect. So he took another, then another... After the third, Eleanor went to find William, since David showed no sign of stopping. A half hour later, he collapsed. No one could wake him up. The twins called their

parents, who told them to call 911 immediately. From then on, every-thing happened really fast. Most people left when they saw things headed downhill. Since I didn't have a ride home, the twins' parents called mine, who came to get me. The trip back was awful, with Mom crying and Dad just driving in total silence.

David was in a coma at the hospital. The pills he'd swallowed weren't ecstasy, but downers. With all the alcohol he'd drunk at the same time, he could have died. They pumped his stomach, and he just barely managed to pull through.

Obviously it didn't end there. The police investigated. All the kids who were at the party had to come with their parents and talk to the cops. They took down the names of people who were drinking and smoking. They said we wouldn't be prosecuted this time, but that if we ever got in trouble again it would be much worse. For William it was a different story. The judge looked at his entire record, the previous con-victions, the rehab programs that had done nothing, the drug treatments he hadn't bothered to finish. The judge told him that the time had come, that he had been given enough chances, and that he was going to be tried for possession and trafficking. I don't know where they are in the trial, but I hope they put him in prison for a long time.

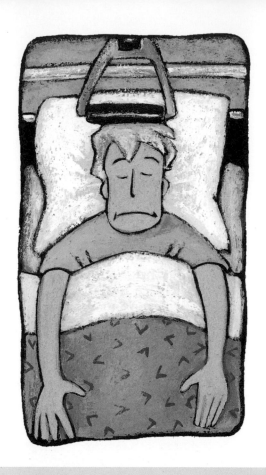

David went back to live with his mother and stepfather. I went to see him while he was in the hospital. He was still really pale and weak. He told me that they were making him go into a drug-treatment program. Eleanor knew that, too. She said that, with any luck, maybe there would be someone there who could actually straighten him out. She wasn't real optimistic, though.

"For rehab to work," she said, "it has to be voluntary. If you're the one who decides to stop using, then it can help. If someone else decides for you, it's no use, it'll never work."

At the end of this horrible year, there was one upside: I actually found a decent friend. I don't know if the word "friend" is exactly right. But after the nightmare party, I felt like I owed something to Eleanor. After all, if she hadn't come up at the right time, I could have had much worse memories than just humiliation and a raging hangover.

I talked about it with Mom, and she told me: "If someone did you a favor, for no apparent reason, with no benefit to herself, the least you can do is to go say thank you." So I got the courage up and went to thank Eleanor. I was stiff and awkward, and she was stunned. She thought that I looked down on her because she was behind in school, which was kind of true. But gradually, we began to talk, and she finally told me what had happened in her life before.

It was a little like David's story. She grew up in a bad part of the city. "There are street kids there," she said, "who get high starting at age ten. When I started smoking pot, I wasn't even thirteen. That's the reason that I can't stand it when someone says it's harmless. Harmless? That's total crap! It cuts you off from reality, it makes you live in a dreamworld. You think you're cool because you don't give a damn about anything. You don't care about school. The screaming matches at home, the stress—that doesn't affect you. You smoke a joint and everything's just . . . cool. But that's the problem. Look at David. He thought he was

really strong. But he barely made it at his last school, he made a mess of the end of the year here; if he continues this way, he'll screw up another year. And all that time, he'll still think he's better than everyone else, like he knows something everybody else doesn't. But it's him who comes off looking stupid. I know what I'm talking about, I've been there."

Eleanor didn't tell me everything. I think she lived through something horrible that she wants to avoid talking about. She let on one day that she had done something really bad that made her wake up: she was in the process of stealing some money from her mother's wallet, and she suddenly saw what she'd become—a thief, a liar, an addict, a girl who didn't care about anything and was headed straight into the gutter. Right then and there she decided to go talk to the counselors at an after-school club in her neighborhood. One of them took her under her wing. She supported her and did everything possible to help her get clean. It wasn't easy, because Eleanor's old friends weren't ready to let her abandon them. Again and again, they took her back down with them. Finally, she realized she would never get out if she stayed in that neighborhood. The counselor knew about the prevention network here. She suggested Eleanor start over here with a clean slate. She'd repeat seventh grade here, staying with friends of the family and going home only for vacations. She jumped at the chance.

"The hardest thing," she confided to me, "has been not having any real friends. Everyone thinks of me as the weird new girl. I feel lonely, especially at night. But I don't want to go back home. I'm scared about what's going to happen this summer. I know I'll run into my old gang again. And when you're surrounded by kids who drink and smoke, it's hard to resist the temptation. I can see myself going back in a bad direction."

"Don't worry," I told her. "I've got an idea."

I can't believe it, but my idea is actually working out. I talked to my parents about Eleanor, and they agreed to act as her guardians for the summer. That means that instead of having to go back to the city and her old life, she can live with us and stay here until school starts again. What's even better is that I convinced Grandma to take her with us on vacation! Every year, we spend three weeks at a cottage in the mountains, where I'm bored out of my mind. It's perfect: if Eleanor goes with us, she won't be tempted to hang out with the potheads in her neighborhood, and I'll have a friend to talk to.

We've made a lot of plans together. She wants to write songs about her experiences. She asked me if I could accompany her on the piano. She has a really good voice, and it turns out I'm not as bad at piano as I thought I was. We've started looking for songs, and we make so much noise that Mom's now nostalgic about the time when I couldn't stand playing. We even managed to work out the chords to that song the band of actors played at the assembly months ago. But we made up a bunch of new, really silly lyrics for it, all about David and William and Karim and Sophie and things we like or hate, that crack us up every time. We'd never let anyone else hear us play—not yet, anyway. But it's so much fun!

2

phase

who should
you believe?

TOBACCO

what should
you do if a
friend is using
drugs?

THE

MARIJUANA

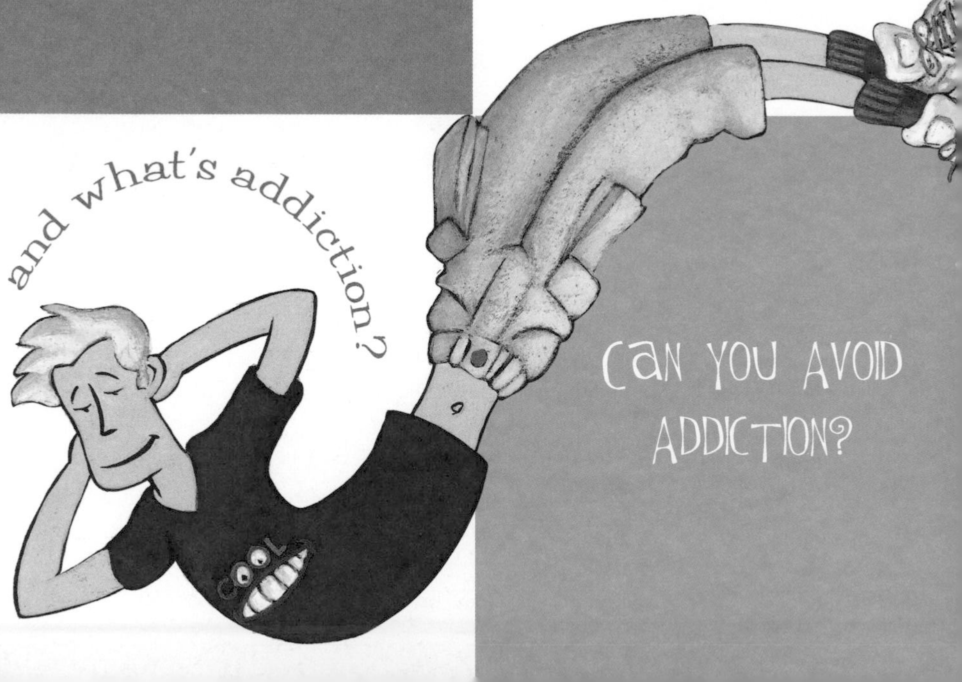

and what's addiction?

CAN YOU AVOID
ADDICTION?

COOL

WHAT DOES IT
FEEL LIKE TO
USE DRUGS?

ALCOHOL

what are drugs, exactly?

how do you know
when someone's
addicted?

BIG QUESTIONS

who should you
believe?

The story you've just read was created from actual cases of real people, as well as the ideas of a psychologist who treats addiction problems. It's possible that the narrator, Emily, is a lot like you. Since she's a teenager who's still very young, Emily is somewhat intrigued by everything she hears about drugs. Yet, at the same time, she doesn't know what to think about it all. Just like Emily, you're probably wondering who to believe—the adults who try to frighten you with horror stories about the effects of drugs, or kids your own age, who, like David, argue that using marijuana is harmless. To form your own conclusions, you need more reliable information, not just people's opinions expressed without any real facts to back them up.

what are drugs,
exactly?

According to the World Health Organization, a drug is a substance, whether natural or synthetic (that is, made artificially in the laboratory), that alters bodily processes. That includes medicines that prevent, cure, or treat diseases. It also includes "psychoactive" or "psychotropic" substances, those that affect mental processes, changing the way your senses work or the way you behave. Some drugs are legal, like the ones you buy at the pharmacy. Others are illegal, like marijuana, cocaine, and heroin.

and what's
addiction?

The human body is like a well-oiled machine: it has its own rhythms and chemical processes, and it works with incredible regularity. If you mess with this consistency—say by smoking cigarettes, drinking alcohol, or taking drugs—the body first rebels in protest, then it adapts to the attack by changing the way it works. It gets used to the new substance, and pretty soon becomes dependent on it.

psychological dependency

There's a risk of psychological dependency in any activity that you do repeatedly. With drugs, psychological dependency means that you can no longer resist the desire to keep taking the drug. You're so used to it that it feels uncomfortable to stop. It becomes a habit, just like biting your nails or cracking your knuckles. This can happen with any drug, even those that people say aren't "addictive."

physical dependency

Some drugs also carry a risk of physical dependency. This means that not only your mind, but your body as well, has become hooked. Even though the drug is harming the body, it can no longer function normally without it. This is especially true of tobacco and heroin: the smoker who's trying to quit and the heroin addict who can't get her fix are in a state of deprivation. They suffer both mental and physical symptoms:

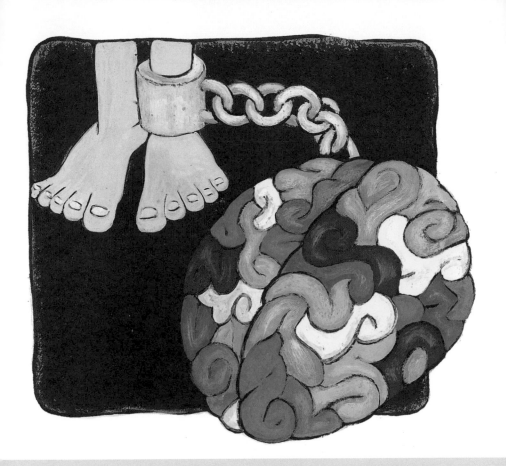

sweats, chills, cramps, stomach pains, agitation, anxiety, and genuine dread. People who are physically dependent on, or addicted to, a drug, often must go through a withdrawal program so that their body can, once again, work effectively without the drug.

withdrawal: learning to live without drugs

Withdrawal is very difficult for the sufferer. But with medical help (and depending on the drug), the worst of the physical symptoms can come and go within in a few days or weeks. On the other hand, psychological withdrawal, the process of breaking the mental habit, can take much longer. In some cases, former addicts struggle with it their whole lives—they're never completely "cured."

no one can be detoxified by force

Regardless of the circumstances, detox (withdrawal, or removal of the drug) is almost never successful unless it's voluntary. This is easy to see in David's and Eleanor's cases. Eleanor realized that she would end up completely wasting her future if she continued to take drugs. She became truly motivated to quit. But even for her, the process wasn't easy. She didn't suffer physical withdrawal symptoms, but she was afraid of giving in to temptation if she returned to an environment where drugs were readily available. David, on the other hand, never thought of giving up drugs. His parents believed they had solved the problem by exiling him to the suburbs and by cutting him off from the "bad influence" of his friends. Unfortunately, though, it was their decision, not his. He wasn't motivated to quit. He easily found new dealers and new friends who were all too similar to the last bunch.

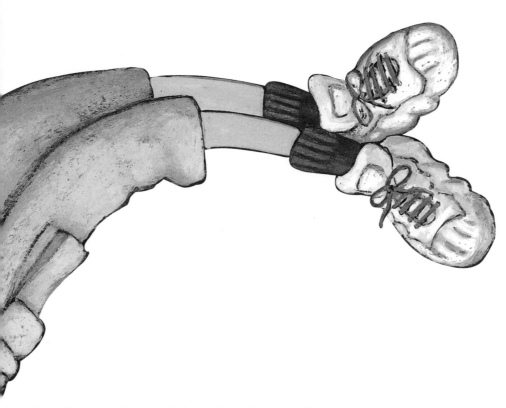

how does psychological dependency take root?

David's attitude is a good example of psychological dependency. For David, marijuana is a tool for relaxation, for feeling cool. If, however, you get used to associating a given substance with a sense of well-being, you run the risk of being unable to get that feeling without the substance. As long as the substance makes you feel happier, more at ease with yourself, more self-confident, you'll have trouble feeling good without it . . . and that's where dependence begins.

can you avoid
addiction?

When it comes to dependency, or addiction, you've probably heard a lot of contradicting opinions. It's possible that you know some-one, either firsthand or through rumors, who smokes marijuana, but hasn't become an addict—they can get high once or twice, and then not do it again for months and they're fine. You may also have been warned: "If you start, you won't be able to stop, and eventually you'll move on to even worse drugs." The problem behind all this is that we're not all affected by drugs in the same exact way, either biologically, socially, or psychologically. All kinds of factors play into the equation; they're the result of genetics as well as personal experience. Some psychologists believe that addiction results from the combination of three things: substance, individual, and sociocultural opportunity.

the three factors that contribute to drug addiction

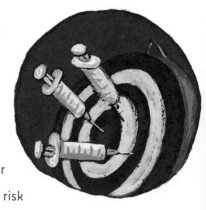

the substance

A substance by itself does not create addiction. If this were true, all Americans who drank even one beer would become alcoholics! Of course, the risk of dependency is dictated by the substance's unique properties. Heroin is known to be extremely physically addictive and to take hold very quickly. But that's not true of marijuana. Caffeine and cocaine are both stimulants, but their strength is completely different: caffeine is to cocaine what a campfire is to the atomic bomb.

the individual

The risk of addiction is also a matter of individual predisposition, or sensitivity. We know that tolerance to alcohol depends on weight (lighter people need fewer drinks to get drunk) and gender (women process alcohol differently and so become drunk more quickly than men). A glass of vodka and orange juice will not have the same effect on Emily, who weighs, at most, a hundred pounds, as it does on an adult male who weighs twice that.

Psychological makeup is another determining factor. In the story, for example, David and Eleanor's lives have been much harder than Emily's. David doesn't get along with his stepfather and goes to a school where he gets little guidance. Eleanor describes her home life as hellish, without giving too many more details. For both of them, drugs held the illusion of a way out, a way to escape a painful or unbearable reality. Emily's life is completely different: even though she complains about boredom, her family is close and loving and her parents are willing to offer guidance—she has little motivation to turn to drugs.

But just to be clear: while a difficult personal situation may add greater risk, there is nothing inevitable about the decision to take drugs! The fact that a person grew up in a bad neighborhood or an abusive family does not mean that she will necessarily end up with a syringe in her arm. Proof of this lies in the fact that brothers and sisters raised in the same house and in the same environment often develop very different personalities. Remember Karim and his brother, Mustapha? Mustapha chose to do drugs, and ended up becoming an addict and dying from an overdose, while Karim, even though he went through some difficult times, succeeded in overcoming the obstacles in his life and making good decisions. He even used his experiences to help others.

the opportunity

Finally, the third major factor in determining whether someone becomes an addict: the opportunity. To do drugs, you have to be able to get drugs, to be around people who have them. Not too many people get smashed for the first time just sitting in their bedroom by themselves. Instead, like Emily, they do it at a party where there are a bunch of people trying to have a good time. In that case, it's often curiosity or wanting to experience new sensations that motivates them to experiment with drugs. And that's not even taking into account the desire to be like everyone else, to not be a baby who drinks fruit juice while the others have already graduated to beer. For some people, the first time will be the last. For others, there'll be a next time, and a next, and a next.

You could also take "opportunity" to mean an event or an experience that prompts someone to turn to drugs. It could be a breakup with a boyfriend or girlfriend, another bad report card, a death in the family, a divorce. These are all things that make people vulnerable even though they might not be aware of it. Drugs might seem like a temporary remedy for sadness, frustration, anger, or hurt. Drinking or taking something might let you forget about your problems for a few hours, but unfortunately it won't solve them, and it often creates brand-new problems or makes the existing ones worse.

Again, nothing is absolutely fated to happen. But every addiction starts with a first time. Only a small number of people who have smoked marijuana will go on to more dangerous drugs; still, most addicts say they started with marijuana.

At this point you might be wondering what kind of experience you would have if you ever tried drugs. No one can tell you with any certainty. People spend their entire lives learning about their personalities, their bodies, and their limits. During adolescence, you're still figuring out who you are. Some psychologists compare these years to the time when a lobster is between two moltings: you've shed your youthful shell, but your new adult one hasn't grown in yet. And that makes you especially vulnerable.

To test yourself, to take risks, is a fundamental part of life. You have to be able to distinguish, though, between the risks that are worth it, the ones you can handle—trips to exotic places, rock climbing, performing on stage as a musician or actor—and other risks that put way too much at stake. If you jump on a motorcycle going a hundred miles per hour without a helmet or any training, the odds are much greater that you'll wake up in the hospital—if you wake up at all—than that you'll impress everyone with your daring.

what does it feel like to use
drugs?

You've heard about hard drugs like heroin or amphetamines, but you're probably most curious right now about the less deadly substances, the ones you've actually seen people use. Maybe you're wondering what it feels like when you smoke cigarettes or pot, or drink beer. Maybe you're telling yourself: "After all, if people take drugs, they must be getting something out of it." What exactly that is depends on the specific drug.

tobacco

It's possible that you've already taken a drag on a cigarette—even though it's illegal to sell cigarettes to anyone under age eighteen. If so, you were probably disappointed with the result: no big change, no feeling like you're master of the universe, no high. At most, your head spins for a few moments, there's a strange taste in your mouth, and you feel a little dizzy. That is, unless you happened to be among the few who also got totally nauseated. If, as sometimes happens, you threw up yesterday's lasagna, or practically coughed up a lung—that's actually a good thing. You're probably not going to go back for a second drag, and chances are you'll never repeat the experiment. If you do keep smoking, though, soon you'll no longer even feel that spinning and dizziness. What will you feel? Nothing much at all. But don't despair! If you force yourself to smoke regularly, after a few months the effects will get a lot more interesting—say, when you go on vacation with your parents and can't sneak any cigarettes for a week. You'll be in a nasty mood, you'll start to fantasize about picking up butts up off the street, you'll spend time coming up with excuses for why you need to run over to the corner store—alone. And, at night, you'll hang out the window like a contortionist so you can secretly smoke while Mom and Dad are busy in the bathroom brushing their teeth. Tobacco has the dubious distinction of being a substance that brings barely any noticeable pleasure, but causes intense withdrawal as soon as you try to stop. It's also one of the worst things you can put into your body. It slowly but relentlessly destroys your lungs and leads to things like cancer, heart disease, and emphysema, to name just a few. About one-third of young smokers will eventually die of smoking-related diseases—that's about one out of every three smokers!

the influence of others: smoking to belong

So why does anyone smoke, then? The answer is simple: people smoke because tobacco is one of the most addictive substances we know of. Once you start, it can be difficult to stop, even if you started for a lame reason. People sometimes start smoking during adolescence to show that they're not little kids anymore. They want to seem older, and to be part of a group ritual. In fact, teenagers often pass a cigarette around a circle of people. It takes a lot of strength to refuse the collective drag that brings the group together. But it's worth it. Some teens, especially girls, smoke to suppress their appetites and lose weight. This is just another way of trying to belong—trying to meet some social ideal of thinness, and it's just about as smart as cutting off an arm to shed a few pounds. The damage is there; it's just on the inside where the smoker can't see it.

Despite all the informational campaigns that trumpet tobacco's negative health effects, it's still a relatively accepted drug. As a smoker, there's less chance of being labeled a social misfit than there is for users of other drugs. Adults can smoke on the street without getting nasty looks, or getting arrested. Tobacco doesn't prevent people from working, keeping up a conversation, following the rules of good manners and life in society. While a smoker's morning breath might be pretty nasty, it's not destroying the rainforest or causing wars. But that's where our praise for smoking ends. If you're still not convinced and you still feel the need to hold something smoldering in your fingers when hanging out with the gang, here's our advice: instead of smoking, burn a five-dollar bill. The effect on your finances will be the same, and your teeth will stay white, your lungs pink.

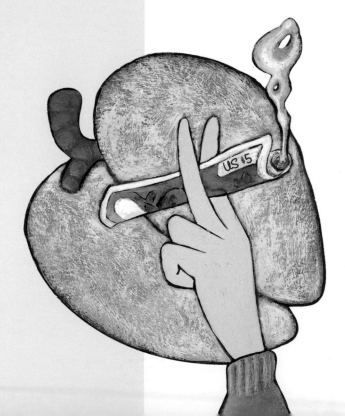

alcohol

Alcohol is pretty widely used in America and throughout the world. For adults who drink it in moderation, it can actually provide some health benefits. But it can be extremely danger-ous as well.

alcohol and american culture

It's legal for people aged twenty-one or older to drink, and alcohol is a part of life for most adults: Wine enthusiasts talk about bouquet and body and have the classification of all the vari-ous vintages down to a science; our dads have a couple of beers while watching the game; our aunts and uncles go out for cocktails after work; our grandparents have a gin and tonic every day at five p.m. like clockwork. You may have even had a celebratory sip of champagne at a cousin's wedding, or your graduation to seventh grade, or the first time you got a decent grade in math.

When it's not abused, alcohol promotes sociability. That is, it puts people at ease and relaxes them. But have one drink too many and relaxed becomes tipsy, and tipsy becomes out-of-it, and out-of-it becomes out-of-control. It's difficult to tell where the line is between relaxed and trashed—especially when you're somewhere between the two, and especially when you're young.

alcohol is a hard drug

Unfortunately, when drunk to excess, alcohol is also an especially devastating drug. To see the potential effects, just think about how many homeless people on the street have bottles in their hands. People who are drunk often aren't aware of the way they're acting. They lose all sense of limits. They make a spectacle of themselves, slurring their speech, bursting into sobs or insults, and sometimes becoming aggressive or violent. If they drink enough, they can get alcohol poisoning and end up in a coma. When a drinker becomes an alcoholic, he or she experiences physical and psychological dependency, and it's very difficult to quit. When they do get things under control, most can't ever let themselves have another sip of alcohol for the rest of their lives, for fear they'll plummet right back to where they were before. Since alcohol makes you lose your self-control, your professional life is compromised, and the repercussions for family life can be catastrophic.

a deadly pairing: alcohol and the road

Even when a person hasn't had that much to drink, alcohol greatly increases the risk of car accidents. For some people (depending on body size and other factors), just a couple of drinks puts them over the legal limit for driving. First, drunkenness decreases the sense of balance and impairs the reflexes; second, it gives people a sense of power and invincibility—they think, "I'm fine! Nothing's going to happen to me! I can handle it." All too often, young people leave a party or a club after a night of drinking and drive away at full speed, thinking they're just a little tipsy, no big deal. Until a bend in the road comes out of nowhere and sends them flying into a tree.

alcohol: some practical advice

It's unlikely that you'll manage to go through your whole life without ever having a drink. Just remember that alcohol has the potential to be dangerous, and keep in mind this advice to prevent the worst case scenario:

• Avoid mixing drinks. At a party where several types of alcohol are being served, don't taste some of everything. Wine + vodka + gin + punch + beer = guaranteed nausea and a massive hangover the next day. If you drink, keep to a single kind of alcohol. Your liver will be forever grateful.

• Watch out for alcohol mixed into other beverages, like soda and fruit

juice. These drinks will go down as easily as water, putting you at risk of ingesting a whole lot of alcohol in a small amount of time—you won't know what hit you. (This is what happened to Emily, who suffered the consequences.)

• Avoid people who push you to drink. "Oh, come one, just one beer! It won't kill you. What, are you just going to drink milk all night?" These people aren't really concerned about your well-being. For whatever reason, they just want to get you drunk. Which has to make you wonder why—so you can entertain everyone by making a fool of yourself? So you'll make out with someone you ordinarily wouldn't?

• Finally, don't trust yourself! You under the influence of alcohol are not the same as you under normal conditions. Maybe your everyday self is shy and reserved, but alcohol removes inhibitions. This may seem nice at the time, but it creates problems the next day when your buddies recount all the misadventures you have no memory of. When you find out you did a striptease in public, or you hung all over a guy or girl you barely know, or you threw up on your best friend's bed—or all three, as the case may be—you probably won't feel very proud of yourself.

marijuana

Here's a drug that's actually illegal—for everyone that is, not just for minors. Smoking it will do similar, if not worse, damage to your lungs as tobacco, but it's effect on your state of mind is much more noticeable.

Marijuana is a plant that is dried and then either rolled up in paper like a cigarette or put into a pipe and smoked. It can also be eaten. Its effects will be stronger or weaker depending on its source and its percentage of THC, or tetrahydrocannabinol, the active ingredient.

Like alcohol, marijuana produces a feeling of euphoria. The relaxation it brings sometimes translates into attacks of insane giggling. The joint smoker will crack up at anything—everything seems funny. His senses are intensified: smells and tastes seem stronger, more distinct, more "saturated" than usual—which often results in an eating binge known as "the munchies." Smoking pot also makes your mouth go all dry and pasty.

Unfortunately, the hilariously comical and great-tasting world of the pothead isn't real. While he feels like he's achieved a superior plane of well-being, the clear-eyed observer sees a dazed druggy with bloodshot eyes and coordination problems, who loses his train of thought way too much.

But maybe you're thinking, hey, if the person who's doing it feels good and doesn't care how other people see him, then what's the harm?

the hidden danger of marijuana: apathy

One of the problems is that excessive use of marijuana makes people apathetic; in other words, they have no energy. It offers a dangerous escape from reality for vulnerable people, especially during adolescence. Joints lead to daydreams and delusions, not to action. They don't make you strong or creative or intelligent, although it might seem that way temporarily. Musicians sometimes think they play better when they're high, but their sober audience doesn't necessarily agree.

Marijuana saps a person's capacity to motivate herself to do anything. Heavy smokers end up feeling that nothing is worth the effort of making an effort. They're at their best laid out on the couch, very busy dreaming of the great things they'll accomplish when the next five minutes are up—that is, after the next joint, or maybe the one after that, or the one after that. They'll do their homework later. They'll apply for after-school jobs later. They'll help raise money for the class trip to Disney World later. But then, they'd have to get up—what a drag! Is that stuff really important anyway? After all, life's just fine right here in front of the TV. The trip probably wouldn't be as cool as just sitting around all week. Isn't it better daydreaming life away than living it?

marijuana and failure at school

The continuous use of a substance that encourages laziness doesn't mesh well with being a student. Incapable of getting down to work, marijuana users lose all interest in school. They complete fewer and fewer assignments, cut classes more and more often . . . the result isn't hard to imagine. In Emily's story, David's actions are a good example of this kind of attitude, which is especially hard to remedy because the person himself usually fails to see the problem. He refuses to admit that it's not entirely normal to be so unmotivated, and to feel good only when you're in a daze.

club drugs

The term "club drugs" usually refers to four substances: ecstasy (or MDMA), GHB, rohypnol, and ketamine. They got their name because they're most popular at dance clubs and rave parties. Ecstasy and GHB are the most common of the four. Ecstasy is a stimulant that comes in pill form. People take it so they can keep dancing all night, or because it reduces inhibitions and tends to make them really touchy-feely. Unfortunately, it can also cause severe dehydration and make your body temperature skyrocket. Transfixed by the sights and sounds and feel of dancing, ecstasy users aren't thinking about stopping for a drink of water or some fresh air. That's why using ecstasy even one time could be deadly—the drug has been linked to seizures, strokes, and liver, kidney, and cardiovascular failure.

GHB is often taken as a clear liquid, but it also comes in powder or pill form. When it's dissolved in a drink, it becomes pretty much taste-less. That, unfortunately, makes it popular as a "date rape drug," meaning one that someone slips into the drink of another person in

order to take advantage of him or her. It makes the user super-relaxed and out-of-it, so she's less likely (or able) to object to what's happening to her, and may affect her memory of the experience later on. Another big problem with GHB: concentrations vary widely, so it's easy to take too much. Overdosing on GHB can depress your lungs so much that they stop working, putting you into a coma.

how do you know when someone's
addicted?

After all we've just said, you're probably asking yourself where the boundary lies between occasional use of a substance and true addiction. Not all people who drink alcohol are alcoholics, just as not all pot smokers are walking shipwrecks. So where do you draw the line?

Since each person and situation is different, there's no absolute, concrete answer. But here are some guidelines.

"recreational" use

When someone smokes cigarettes or drinks alcohol only now and then, it's called "recreational" use, meaning it's limited to specific occasions and tends not to have serious repercussions on the rest of the person's life. It's recreational when, for example, someone at a party drinks enough to become a little less inhibited, without getting completely wasted.

abuse

Abuse starts when the user stops limiting his drug use to just "now and then." An abuser may not drink every day, but he doesn't stop once the beverages start flowing. In other people, abuse is sneakier—they might not even seem drunk or high, but when's the last time you saw them without a drink or a joint in their hand?

drug addiction

The true drug addict has lost all ability to moderate her consumption. Even though she may be aware of the harmfulness of the substance, she can no longer do without it. The drug becomes a "psychological crutch."

She may not feel good anymore when she drinks or shoots up, but she feels awful when she doesn't.

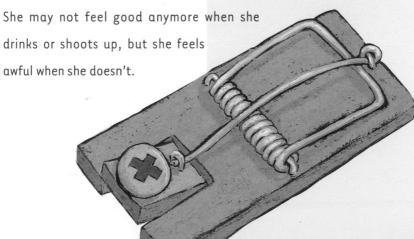

drugs and delinquency

Little by little, the addict's preoccupation with drugs takes precedence over every other concern. The only thing that matters to him is the next fix. Any scheme or plan seems justified to him, as long as it helps him get the money he needs to buy the drug. Eleanor admits that she stole money from her mom's purse. Alex did the same thing. To a greater or lesser extent, and with greater or lesser severity, addiction leads to delinquency when it creates a need that can never be fully satisfied.

the addict denies reality

In many instances, the drug addict refuses to admit he's addicted. He's convinced he can stop whenever he wants to; the problem being, of course, that he never wants to. Or, to be more precise, there's always some outside circumstance that prevents him from acting on his promises to quit. Alcoholics are great at this: it's a sure thing, tomorrow they'll stop drinking. But today, as it turns out, there's a birthday to celebrate, or an office party to attend, and so on. Tomorrow, though,

don't worry, he'll stop, and he'll do it with one hand behind his back! But the people around him have heard it all before. They know he never follows through. It's no use trying to make him feel ashamed, or appealing to his willpower or conscience. If he could solve his problem by himself, he wouldn't be an addict. Once he agrees to face reality, it's best to advise him to seek professional help and to avoid situations where he'll be tempted to return to his habit. When someone wants to quit drinking or smoking, the last thing he needs is bunch of friends offering him a beer or a cigarette.

what should i do if a friend is using
drugs?

If you know someone who you think might have a problem, what can you do? Some kids say: "I'm not going to tell anyone. I'd be betraying my buddy." But others say: "I'd tell right away."

Some secrets and confidences are too heavy to bear. If you know that a friend is putting her life in danger, you can't keep it to yourself. Whether it's drugs or a suicide threat, it's extremely serious.

the worst solution of all: act as though nothing's wrong

So what can you actually do? First, try to talk to your friend about it, encourage her to open up to an adult, and suggest that you'll go with her. Maybe all she needs is your support to make up her mind.

look for a trustworthy person you can talk to

If your friend refuses to get help, you'll have to take matters into your own hands. Tell someone you trust and respect: it might be your father, your mother, a school nurse, a teacher, or a youth worker. It doesn't matter whether that person specializes in drug treatment or not. The main thing is to choose wisely: this information could have huge consequences, so you need to find someone who you think will know the right thing to do. Not all adults know how to handle situations like this. For example, if your friend has horrible fights with her parents almost every day, they probably aren't the best choice. If a school principal has the right to expel your friend for whatever she's into, he might not be the best choice. That said, there are plenty of people to turn to who will be more than willing to help.

should they be legalized?

THE DRUG

APPENDICES

...BUT IT'S THE LAW

who are you?

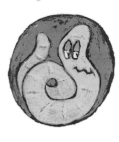

DEBATE

THE LAW IS HARSH . . .

should they be
legalized?

Some people think that all drugs should be made legal. They believe it should be left up to each person to exercise responsibility for his or her own actions. Others think the opposite, that all drugs should be illegal. They believe that it's the government's job to protect people who otherwise wouldn't protect themselves.

Societies have been declaring psychotropic substances legal or illegal for a long time. For example, here in the United States in the 1920s, alcohol was made illegal—this period was called Prohibition. The upshot? It didn't work very well. Alcohol consumption didn't decrease, people just drank bootleg (or illegal) liquor in secret, making average citizens into criminals and making gangsters, like Al Capone, who sold the stuff, rich. When prohibition was lifted, people could drink openly again—and they did. So in the end, neither banning alcohol nor lifting the ban solved the problem of alcoholism.

what's the position of those who want to legalize drugs?

Those who support legalization often point to the failure of Prohibition
as an example of their argument. Their view is that the people who want
to take drugs will do it anyway, and that these people face more risk,
not less, when drugs are illegal, because they're forced to buy drugs
from criminals. In Emily's story, this is the argument that David uses
during the debate at school: beginning with his belief that marijuana is
not dangerous, he argued for its legalization so that people would not
be forced to go to irresponsible drug dealers who could sell kids even
more dangerous substances.

and what do their opponents say?

The opponents of legalization believe that no drug is harmless, and making access to drugs easier is not the way to combat their use. They also argue that the fact that a certain type of behavior is widespread is not a good reason to make it legal. For example, a lot of people don't obey the speed limit, but no one is asking that these limits be done away with.

In reality, society tries to maintain the right balance between the psychotropic substances that are permitted and controlled (like morphine, for example, used as a painkiller in hospitals) and those that are banned outright (like marijuana and cocaine). The laws aren't perfect, but they're the ones democratic societies like ours have freely enacted for themselves, and they apply to everyone equally. No law fits every single person perfectly; what counts, though, is that they're the same for every person. There may be societies without justice, but there's never been justice without society.

the law
is harsh . . .

We Americans are lucky to live in a democracy. We obey the laws that are enacted by senators and representatives freely elected by voters. It bears repeating: we're fortunate. Think of the countries where people are controlled by dictators, army generals, or violent political parties. In the U.S., no citizen is above the law, not even the president. So far, we've talked about a number of substances that could be abused and/or cause addiction. We mentioned tobacco, alcohol, and marijuana, among others. So what is the status of these substances in the eyes of the law?

Tobacco manufacture and sales are tightly controlled. However, cigarettes are legal, as long as they're sold by licensed people to customers over the age of eighteen. In recent years, many states have banned smoking in certain areas, such as post offices, town halls, and other public buildings, and in restaurants and bars. These laws have been enacted to protect nonsmokers from the harmful effects of breathing in secondhand smoke.

The manufacture and sale of alcohol, like tobacco, is also very closely regulated. While brewing beer or making wine at home is legal, making large quantities of liquor is not. People under age twenty-one cannot purchase alcohol, and bartenders are not allowed to serve it to them. Stores and bars check the IDs of young-looking customers because they can get in serious trouble for selling alcohol to those who are underage.

Not all types of alcohol are legal in the U.S., even for adults. Making and selling absinthe was prohibited in 1912. This anise-flavored liquor popular with writers and artists around the end of the nineteenth century was thought to drive drinkers literally insane

the current laws

Substances such as marijuana, heroin, cocaine, and ecstasy appear on a list of "scheduled drugs," meaning the government has classified them according to their medicinal value, harmfulness, and potential for abuse and addiction. The Controlled Substances Act of 1970 created these schedules and allows the government to regulate the manufacture and distribution of the scheduled drugs. Schedule 1 is where the most dangerous drugs are listed, the ones that have no recognized medical use, while Schedule 5 is home to the least dangerous drugs. The law allows drug users to be punished for their offenses, but it may also dictate that the offender get treatment for his or her addiction.

The use of marijuana, ecstasy, cocaine, heroin—and many other kinds of drugs—is a crime.

The maximum penalties for people who break drug laws vary from state to state. They also vary by the amount and type of drug involved. In most states, the maximum penalty for marijuana possession is a year

in prison and/or up to a $5,000 fine. For harder drugs like cocaine, maximum penalties range from one to twenty-five years in prison and/or up to a $500,000 fine. Maximum penalties for selling drugs are almost always higher than for just possessing them.

Some states have strict minimum penalties as well. However, in many states and cases, the judge can decide whether a punishment should be harsher or more lenient depending on the circumstances, such as whether the person is a first-time offender. If so, the sentence is likely to be less severe than those listed above. The judge may also order the offender to be placed in a drug rehabilitation program, or go to a special medical clinic, doctor, or psychologist who can help treat the addiction.

Like possession and sale, the production or manufacture of illegal substances (for example, growing marijuana plants) and the operation and organization of drug rings (groups of people that work together to obtain and sell drugs) are also crimes.

Adults today find it difficult to talk about rules. Some parents don't want to forbid things; they'd rather act like friends or buddies to their kids, hoping that this will help them have a better relationship. Many of them may have experimented with drugs themselves

when they were young. Some may still do drugs now, and not always hide it from their kids. So it's no wonder making your own decisions about this stuff isn't easy. And that's why, despite all the debate, it's a pretty good thing that we have laws to guide us

laws are necessary

Rules don't exist just to get in the way of your fun. First and foremost, they're a contract, an agreement between people, a compromise that allows humans to live together in a community. You could even view rules as a sign of love. Most rules are designed to protect you, so they're a sign that someone worries about you and cares what happens to you. After all, when you love someone, you don't just watch as they hurt themselves, sitting idly by and saying, "Hey, doesn't matter, do whatever you want."

law

laws weren't created out of thin air

The laws of society may prove more or less effective once they're in place. But they don't just come out of nowhere. They're made by humans—who, by the way, aren't perfect—for humans, who must live together with their good points and their flaws. Democracy is all about people electing representatives to create the laws that they will then have to obey. Without laws, it would be a world where "might makes right," meaning the strongest person (or the one with the biggest gun) gets his way every time. Anyone could do anything to anyone because there would be no consequences. This sort of thing actually happens sometimes, in dangerous neighborhoods where there aren't enough police, or at the school David used to go to in Emily's story. When there are no laws, innocent people lose much more freedom than they gain. In a democracy, the laws guarantee the rights of every citizen.

So now that we're done singing "God Bless America," let's get back to talking about the big decisions that you'll soon be facing. The biggest, of course, being "Who am I, and what kind of person do I want to be?" These are pretty much the most basic, but most important questions you'll ever ponder. They're questions that you ask yourself now, and that you'll continually ask yourself throughout your entire life. And they're the questions you'll have to keep ready in a corner of your mind for that crucial day when—and if—you're tempted to have a drink or try drugs.

If you ever get it into your head that you want to drink, try a ciga-rette, or experiment with some pill or joint or other substance, before jumping in headfirst, think a couple moves ahead: "Is this my idea, or do I just want to feel like I'm part of the group? If I do this, then there's a strong chance it'll be hard to stop doing it—do I really want to be someone who can't live without alcohol/cigarettes/coke/etc.?" Or worse: "Is there a chance that doing it just this one time could seriously screw up my life—or end it?"

one final word

After reading this book, you're now armed with a whole arsenal of infor-mation. But if you only remember one thing from all the advice that's been passed on, make it this: excess in anything is dangerous. As soon as you start to abuse something—in other words, to do too much of it—that thing becomes harmful. This is true not only of alcohol and tobacco, but also, for example, of eating french fries, watching TV, playing com-puter games—even studying. (Don't tell your parents we said that.)

Someone who brags about how much he can drink shouldn't impress you with his supposed strength and tolerance. He's not strong: he's intoxicated. When the body is able to take in excessive amounts of a substance without showing any visible signs that something's wrong, that just means it's lost its healthy reflexes and can no longer send out the proper warning signals. For most people, smoking a cigarette for the first time makes them feel slightly ill—that's a warning sign. That's how your body tells you that you're doing something harmful to it—just like feeling pain tells you to get your hand off a hot burner. When it comes down to it, this isn't a question of morality or what's right and wrong;

it's a matter of health. If you smoke or drink or do drugs, you must be aware of the risks you're running. And you have to ask yourself: Is this experience worth risking my health—or my life?

who are you?

You'll need your entire life to really and truly answer that question. In the meantime, have some fun and take this mini-quiz: If you were an animal, which one would you be? Read the descriptions below, then pick the one that sounds most like you and how you operate with others. Or, better yet, decide which one you want to be and then be it. Will you be...

The sheep: I stick with the herd. I'm not good at saying no. I'm scared that my friends will reject me or make fun of me if I don't go along with what they want to do. I don't usually share my opinion or make my voice heard. I don't make waves, I go with the flow.

The lion: I roar. I'm not afraid to say when I disagree with others. I'd rather be all alone than be forced to do anything I don't want to do. I like being part of a pride, but I'm just as happy blazing my own trail. If the others want to come along, that's fine. But first and foremost, I look out for number one.

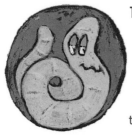

The earthworm: Like fishermen's bait, I love to see whether I can reel people in—hook, line, and sinker. I'm always the first to say: "Bet you can't drink one more!" or "You should try this stuff, it's top of the line, you'll see . . . "

The nervous pooch: When life gets hard or scary, I'm not strong enough to face it. I run as fast as I can to try to escape. And when my problems catch up to me, I bury my head in my blanket—or smoke, or bottle—and hope that they'll disappear if I just distract myself long enough.

The rescue dog: I'm the best friend you'll ever have, the guardian who never barks except to protect or save someone. I love my friends and I don't want them to lose their way or fall headfirst into the ravine. I'm always the one to rescue a lost friend. As for drugs—no thanks, not for me.

The fox: I'm naturally curious, there's no doubt about that. But I'm also cautious. When you put something appetizing in front of me, I try to think about how it'll all play out before I get my paws too deep in it.

test your
knowledge

	True	False
1. Drugs have always existed.		
2. People have talked about drug addiction since the beginning of time.		
3. The following drugs can cause a coma: A. Alcohol B. Tobacco C. Inhalants D. Heroin E. Ecstasy F. Marijuana		
4. Marijuana carries no risk of dependency.		
5. Using marijuana inevitably leads to the use of other drugs, like cocaine or heroin.		
6. Many drug addicts say they started with marijuana.		
7. Alcohol is a completely legal drug.		
8. You can't be arrested for drinking alcohol.		
9. You can't be arrested for using marijuana.		
10. Quitting drugs is a matter of willpower.		

answers to the test

1. True.

2. False: The words "drug addict" and "drug addiction" first appeared during the last decades of the twentieth century.

3. A. True. B. False. C. True. D. True. E. True . F. False.

4. False.

5. False.

6. True.

7. False.

8. False: Underage drinking and driving while intoxicated are both illegal.

9. False.

10. False: Many drugs cause physical dependency, which usually requires treatment rather than mere willpower.

resources

for more information:

www.teenshealth.org
Info on a number of health topics, including alcohol, tobacco, and drugs.

www.drugfreeamerica.org
Includes a Drug Resources page providing detailed descriptions of nearly forty substances, organized by official names and slang names.

for help finding treatment:

Tobacco
www.ucanbreathe.com
Site developed by former smokers to help others quit.

www.lungusa.org/tobacco
The American Lung Association's stop smoking page.

Alcohol
www.al-anon.alateen.org
Al-anon/Alateen, two programs that help families and friends of alcoholics.

www.alcoholics-anonymous.com
Alcoholics of all ages are welcome at meetings. Find local chapters by looking them up in any phone book.

Drugs
www.samhsa.gov
Substance Abuse and Mental Health Services Administration. For referrals to local drug treatment centers, call 1-800-729-6686.

fyi . . .

Thirteen percent of eighth-graders reported having tried smoking by the fifth grade. More than 10 percent of eighth-graders are current smokers. Nearly 17 percent of tenth-graders are current smokers.

More than a third of all kids who ever try smoking will become regular, daily smokers before leaving high school.

Three out of every four regular smokers in high school have tried to quit, but failed. About one-third of all youth smokers will eventually die prematurely from diseases caused by smoking.

Kids ages twelve to seventeen who smoke are eleven times more likely to use illicit drugs, and sixteen times more likely to drink heavily than kids who don't smoke.

Of all teenagers in grades seven through twelve in America today, 48 percent have tried illegal drugs. Of those teens, 83 percent have tried marijuana.

About 28 percent of teens age twelve to twenty say they use alcohol. Nineteen percent of that group are binge drinkers. Kids who drink before age fifteen are four times more likely to develop alcohol dependence than those who begin drinking at age twenty-one. Over 40 percent of people who start drinking before age thirteen will develop alcohol abuse or dependence at some point in their lives.

In 2002, 29 percent of fifteen- to twenty-year-old drivers killed in motor vehicle crashes had been drinking.

table of principal
drugs

	Drug	Use	Legal Status	Risk of Overdose
I. NARCOTICS	Morphine	Medical/Abuse	Regulated	☠
	Heroin	Abuse	Illegal	☠
	Methadone	Medical/Abuse	Regulated	☠ (in some cases)
II. DEPRESSANTS	Sleeping Pills/ Tranquilizers	Medical/Abuse	Regulated	☠
	GHB	Abuse	Illegal	☠
	Alcohol	Recreational/ Abuse	Regulated	☠
	Inhalants	Household/ Abuse	Legal	☠
III. STIMULANTS	Tobacco	Recreational/ Abuse	Regulated	
	Caffeine	Recreational/ Abuse	Legal	
	Cocaine	Abuse	Illegal	☠
	Crack	Abuse	Illegal	☠
	Ecstasy	Abuse	Illegal	☠
	Crystal Meth	Abuse	Illegal	☠
IV. HALLUCINOGENS	Marijuana/Hashish	Abuse	Illegal	
	Mushrooms	Abuse	Illegal	
	LSD	Abuse	Illegal	
	V. ANABOLIC STEROIDS	Medical/Abuse	Regulated	

attachment to the table

1. Definitions

1.1 *Narcotic:* Drug that soothes, calms, and relaxes—to the extreme.

1.2 *Depressant:* Drug that soothes, calms, and relaxes the user's body and brain.

1.3 *Stimulant:* Drug that excites the brain and body, often causing the user to forget fatigue, hunger, sleepiness.

1.4 *Hallucinogen:* Drug that alters mood and perception (not all hallucinogens cause hallucinations).

1.5 *Anabolic Steroid:* Drug closely related to the male sex hormone testosterone, used for medical purposes and abused by athletes and bodybuilders to enhance performance.

2. Clarifications

Methadone is a medication prescribed for drug addicts as a substitute for heroin.

3. Classification Limits

3.1 Cocaine is technically classified as a narcotic (I), but its effects are more similar to stimulants (III).

3.2 Tobacco stimulates brain activity (III), but some people use it for relaxation (II).

3.3 Depending on the time, the amount ingested, and the person who drinks it, alcohol may cause euphoria, stimulation, and aggressiveness (III); or sleep (II).

bibliography

Magazine articles

Formichelli, Linda. "Why Our Ancestors Said Yes to Drugs: Psychotropics as Sustenance Not Escape." *Psychology Today*, July-August 2002.

Web articles

Libaw, Oliver. "White Lightning Strikes Again: Age-Old Tradition of Moonshine Is Still a Problem." *abcnews.com*, April 9, 2002. *abcnews.go.com/sections/us/DailyNews/moonshine020409.html*

"The Controlled Substances Act." The U.S. Drug Enforcement Agency. *www.usdoj.gov/dea/agency/csa.htm*

Web sites

Al-Anon/Alateen
www.al-anon.alateen.org/

The American Lung Association—Tobacco Control
www.lungusa.org/tobacco/

Campaign for Tobacco-Free Kids®
www.tobaccofreekids.org

The Center for Disease Control—State Laws on Tobacco Control
www.cdc.gov/epo/mmwr/preview/mmwrhtml/ss4803ar.htm

Mothers Against Drunk Driving
www.madd.org

Parents. The Anti-Drug
www.theantidrug.com

Partnership for a Drug-Free America®
www.drugfreeamerica.org

TeensHealth—Drugs and Alcohol
www.teenshealth.org/teen/drug_alcohol

The Robert Wood Johnson Foundation—Study of Illicit Drug Policies
http://www.rwjf.org/publications/publicationsPdfs/drug_policies_report.pdf

Ucanbreathe.com
www.ucanbreathe.com

The U.S. Department of Health and Human Services and SAMHSA's National
Clearinghouse for Alcohol and Drug Information
www.health.org/nongovpubs

The U.S. Department of Health and Human Services and SAMHSA Office
of Applied Studies—2001 National Household Survey on Drug Use
www.samhsa.gov/oas/NHSDA

The U.S. Drug Enforcement Administration Web Site
www.usdoj.gov/dea/

The World Health Organization Lexicon of Alcohol and Drug Terms
www.who.int/substance_abuse/terminology/who_lexicon/en/

index

about the authors

Pierre Mezinski works with troubled young people. Since 1983, he has written about drug abuse and other topics for adults and teenagers. This is his first book in the **sunscreen** series.

Melissa Daly is a former senior staff writer at *Seventeen* magazine, where she wrote articles and columns on health, sexuality, relationships and other topics of interest to teenagers. She is currently an editor at *Fitness* magazine. She is a graduate of the College of William & Mary, and lives in New York City.